A Dorling Kindersley Book

Text Christopher Maynard
Project Editor Caroline Bingham
Art Editor Claire Penny
Deputy Managing Art Editor Jane Horne
Deputy Managing Editor Mary Ling
Production Ruth Cobb
Consultant Theresa Greenaway
Picture Researcher Tom Worsley

Additional photography by Max Gibbs, Steve Gorton, Frank
Greenaway, Dave King, Susannah Price, Pete Gardner, Tim Ridley,
David Rudkin, Clive Streeter, Philip Dowell

First published in Great Britain in 1997
by Dorling Kindersley Limited,
9 Henrietta Street, London WC2E 8PS

Visit us on the World Wide Web at http://www.dk.com

A CIP catalogue record for this book is available from
the British Library.

ISBN: 0-7513-5515-1

Colour reproduction by Chromagraphics, Singapore
Printed and bound in Italy by L.E.G.O.

The publisher would like to thank the following for their kind
permission to reproduce their photographs:

t top, b bottom, l left, r right, c centre, BC back cover, FC front cover

Bruce Coleman Collection: Nick de Vore 14bl, 18-19c; **James Davis:**
10-11c; **The Image Bank:** G Brimacombe 8-9c; **Images Colour Library:**
13cr, 17tr, 20cl; **The National Trust:** Ian Shaw 7tr;
Pictor International: 12-13c;
Rex Features: 12bl; **Tony Stone Images:** 20-21c, BC cb, Lori Adamski
Peek 16-17c, Martin Barraud 15br, John Lawrence 6-7c, Dennis O'Clair
21tr, James Randklev 9br, World Perspectives 15cr;
Telegraph Colour Library: FC cb, 14-15c, endpapers

Contents

WHY

are there waves?

Questions children ask about water

DK

DORLING KINDERSLEY

London • New York • Stuttgart • Moscow

628.1 (E)

All objects reflect light into our eyes so we can see them. When sunlight is reflected off trees onto a still lake, the light rays bounce off the water, producing a clear image just like a mirror.

Why do we need water?
All living things need wate
It's the main ingredient of
plants and animals – in fac

mirror?

Why do rivers always flow the same way?
Since water can't run uphill, every single river in the world must flow downhill towards the lowest place it can find – the sea.

our body is about 60% water. Without water lants soon wilt and die, and so would you. ach day your body loses about 2.5 litres of ater, so it needs to be topped up regularly.

Water is made up of particles called molecules. When you heat water, the molecules begin to move around. The hotter it gets, the faster they move – some even escape into the air, or vaporise, as hot steam.

Why does glass steam up?
When warm, moist air, such as your breath, hits cold glass it cools quickly. The vaporised

turn to steam?

Why does boiling water bubble?
If water is heated to 100°C, it starts to boil and turn into steam. This happens so fast on the heated bottom of a pan that the steam makes a trail of bubbles as it rises through the water.

ater turns back into liquid ater, forming mist on the lass. Dew on grass is also nade from moisture in the air.

When water cools to 0°C, the tiny, bustling molecules that make up water slow down so much that they stick together and the water becomes solid. This is called ice.

Why don't fish freeze in icy water?
Ice is lighter than water and it floats to the surface of a freezing pond. The water below

freeze?

Why is ice sticky?
Really cold ice cubes
from a deep freezer
can freeze the thin
layer of moisture
on your fingertips
as you touch
them. For a
sticky instant,
you and the
cubes are
frozen together!

stays several degrees above
freezing, and that's quite
comfortable for
freshwater fish.

Why do pebbles

If you drop a pebble in a pond, each ripple you see is a tiny wave, set off by the impact of the pebble hitting the water. Ripples happen because water is a liquid.

Why do rivers flood?
When snow melts, or after heavy storms, water

make ripples?

Why are rivers so curvy?
If land was smooth, rivers would run downhill in straight lines. But land is bumpy, with rocks and hills, so rivers wind around to find the easiest path to the sea.

an pour into a river much faster than the river an carry it away. The river begins to rise, and nay even burst its banks and flood the land nearby.

Waves are made by the wind. When wind blows over water, it pushes it up into little waves. In strong winds, the little waves soon build up and can grow as big as hills.

Why is the sea so salty?
Rivers flow down towards the sea. On their way they collect small amounts of

waves?

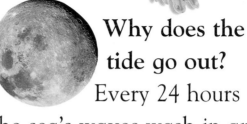

Why does the tide go out?
Every 24 hours the sea's waves wash in and out twice. These tides are controlled by the Moon – as it circles the Earth, the Moon's gravity tugs the sea to and from the shore, like a giant magnet in the sky.

sediment and minerals, such as salt, and deposit them in the sea. Over millions of years the seas have become more and more salty.

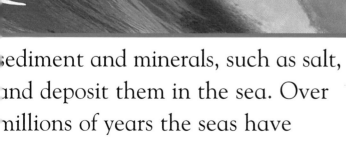

When you get hot, tiny sweat glands in your skin leak drops of salty water. These quickly evaporate, cooling you down by removing heat.

Why does my skin wrinkle in the bath?
After some time in the bath, the top layers of your skin begin to soak up water. As they do they swell, like a grain of rice, and become wrinkled and bumpy.

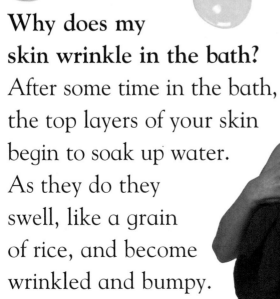

when I run?

Why does my mouth water?
When your brain knows it's time to eat, it tells your mouth to get ready by making lots of watery saliva to help you chew and to start the digestion process.

Why don't camels need

A camel is good at conserving water because the hump on its back stores fluids. It also has a huge stomach – when thirsty, a camel can drink about 114 litres of water at once.

Why can some creatures walk on water?
The surface of water seems to have a kind of elastic skin.

Why doesn't a cactus plant need much water?

A cactus can go for weeks without rain by storing water in its thick, fleshy stems. Instead of leaves that might dry out quickly in the sunshine, cacti have prickles.

This skin effect is called surface tension. Small, light insects can walk on the skin, but you are too heavy and will fall through.

Why can't I breathe

Fish can breathe underwater because they have gills, which let water in and out, and filter oxygen from it. But you have lungs which

Why do I float better in seawater?
Seawater contains lots of salt, so it is denser than the water in a swimming pool or lake, and can support more of your weight.

underwater?

only breathe air. If you
tried to breathe like a
fish, you would drown.

Why do people wear goggles?

If you like to keep your eyes open
underwater, goggles protect them
from chlorine and salt, which
can sting. They also help
you see more clearly.